Once upon a time, enormous herds of wild horses roamed many parts of the earth. Few of them survive today. Only in Africa can we see large numbers of this family, in the shape of zebras, their distinctive black and white stripes as individual to them as fingerprints are to us.

With the aid of beautiful photographs, Daphne Machin Goodall tells the story of the zebra today, the different species, how and where they live, and how they struggle to survive on the African plains.

About the author

Daphne Machin Goodall is well known for her many books on the members of the horse family. She is a member of the Wild Horse Specialist Group and has travelled extensively in her study of wild life. Her translations into English include *The Asiatic Wild Horse* and *Language of the Horse*.

Sir Maurice Yonge, Consultant Editor of Animals of the World, is former Professor of Zoology in the Universities of Bristol and Glasgow.

Animals of the World

Elephants	Edmund Rogers
Lions	Mary Chipperfield
Penguins	Ralph Whitlock
Zebras	Daphne Machin Goodall
Chimpanzees	Ralph Whitlock
Kangaroos	Bernard Stonehouse

SBN 85340 509 3

Printed in England by Loxley Brothers Limited,
Sheffield and London.

Animals of the World
Consultant Editor Sir Maurice Yonge CBE FRS

Zebras

Daphne Machin Goodall

WAYLAND PUBLISHERS ENGLAND

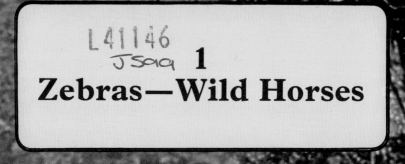

**1
Zebras—Wild Horses**

The wild horse family has many members. There is the Przewalsky wild horse, the onager and kiang, the tarpan and the African ass. The best-known and most beautiful member of the family is the zebra. Its black and white markings make it stand out from the other animals on the plains and mountains of Africa, where it lives. But if you think that all zebras look the same, read on!

No one zebra is striped exactly like another.
Each has a pattern as individual to it as our
fingerprints are to us. This sometimes makes it
hard to tell the various kinds of zebra apart.
There are three main types: Burchell's zebra,
Grévy's zebra and the mountain zebra. The
diagram opposite shows the different markings
of each type. The map shows the areas in Africa
where they live. These are the only places in the
world where they are found.

Above is a Burchell's zebra. There are far
more of this type (about 300,000) than any
other.

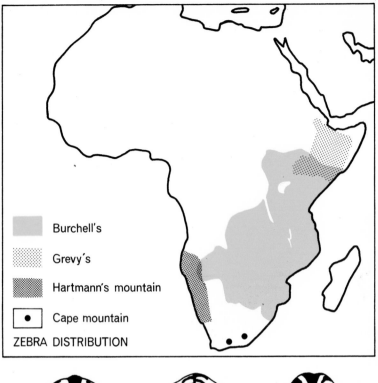

Burchell's

Grevy's

Hartmann's mountain

• Cape mountain

ZEBRA DISTRIBUTION

Grevy's Zebra   Mountain Zebra   Common Zebra

The Burchell zebra has several near relatives. They are not different species, like the mountain and Grévy zebras, but they are marked differently. The Burchell zebra's best known "cousin" is Chapman's zebra. This is also known as the common zebra and is the one we see most often in zoos. These Chapmans are drinking at a water hole with some wildebeeste.

As you can see, they have light shadow stripes between the broader black and white stripes. Their legs are much less striped than those of their larger relative, the Burchell zebra. They have short manes, and sometimes no manes at all. At about 135 cm (4½ ft) tall, they are about the same size as a child's pony.

The Grévy zebra is, in fact, a distant relative of the horse and other zebras. It lives in a small area of Kenya, Ethiopia and the Somali Republic. We call it a zebra simply because it has stripes. Its ancestors may have been the forerunners of the entire horse family. The first horses began to evolve many millions of years ago from extinct animals like the hipparion. The hipparion had three toes and fed on leaves and bushes. During millions of years it evolved into a grazing animal populating steppe, pampas and mountain country. So the zebra was born.

Here is a Grévy zebra. Grévy zebras are the biggest of all the wild horse family. They are a good 150 cm (5 ft) tall. They are also the most aggressive and the least easily tamed. Unlike the other zebras they like being alone, although small groups sometimes graze together as they are doing here. Their long ears are rounded at the tip and their stripes are closer and narrower than those of the common zebra.

Not all the zebras of Africa live on the plains. Here is a group of Hartmann mountain zebras (left). Their stripes do not cover their belly. The Hartmann zebra is a mountain animal. It is agile and can climb steep, rocky places in search of water. These Cape zebras (below) live in the Cape Province mountains of South Africa. There are very few of these zebras left, and they are protected from hunters by law. The Hartmann zebra lives in the mountains along the coastal regions of Angola and Namibia. It too is threatened by extinction.

The mountain zebra is the smallest of the zebra family and stands only about 120 cm (4 ft) high. It looks more like an ass than a horse.

In parts of Africa two types of zebra can be found together in the same herd. They graze together quite happily, although sometimes members of the same species fight with each other.

It is a fine sight to see a herd of zebras galloping across the African plains, like the one in this picture.

2
Life on the Plains

We are now going to look at the life zebras lead on the great plains of Africa. Here, in the early light, they are leaving their night-time resting place. Together they are going in search of fresh savannah grasses and shrubs to eat. As we shall see, they are often accompanied on their wanderings by various other animals.

The zebra's life is ruled by the need for water and grazing. Some days they may travel as much as 50 km (30 miles) in search of food and drink. In the evening they return to the same resting place.

The pace of their life is usually calm. They move at a graceful walk in their constant search for food. Only if they are disturbed or really frightened by predators will they break into a fast gallop. In the picture on the right they stand quite peacefully among the beautiful scenery of their African home.

Chapman's zebras are not territorial. They do not lay claim to a piece of ground which they defend against other herds. But they do have an area they think of as home. The Ngorongoro Crater is one such area. Here the herd can graze over about 260 sq km (100 square miles).

Here we see them drinking in the company of impalas. Zebras prefer to feed on open plains where there is plenty of grass. They often graze with antelope and wildebeeste. Since each animal prefers to eat grasses the others do not like, there are no arguments between them!

At waterholes zebras mix freely with other animals. Their acute hearing and sense of smell make them good "watchdogs". They are always on the alert for enemies and often spot danger before the other animals. As they are not competing for the same food, they can afford to be co-operative.

This zebra (left) is enjoying a good dust-bath. The dust will help it to stay clean and free from lice. The two zebras together (below) are using another method of keeping clean—they are grooming each other's coats. They stand facing each other's tail. Starting at the neck, they nibble vigorously along the withers to the spine. This coat-grooming exercise may last for up to half an hour. It also provides a pleasant massage for the zebras and helps their circulation.

Best of all, though, is a good dip in the water. Like most members of the horse family, zebras enjoy going into the water. Cold water refreshes their tired feet and legs. They may even lie down to bathe.

Like other animals, zebras can communicate with each other. To do so they use their voices and a very expressive sign language. Even at a distance other zebras will notice a particular way of standing and understand its meaning. For instance, a grazing herd will recognize the alertness of these zebras in the picture. Raised ears and heads may indicate danger at hand. They may have picked up the scent of a lion hiding in the bushes. They and their grazing companions are ready to flee.

When one zebra meets another, be they strangers or old friends, they greet each other by sniffing noses and perhaps other parts of the body. This is their way of shaking hands and saying "How do you do?" A similar greeting is given by a stallion interested in a mare. She may reject his advances with an angry squeal or by striking out with a forefoot.

The tone of a zebra's call varies. Sometimes it lets out a loud "qua-ha" sound, sometimes a deep hoarse grunt. It can also make a short whistle. The sounds range in intensity according to each animal's voice. Probably they use a low whisper to their young foals, as horses do, to express affection.

3
Zebra Families

Zebras lead a herd life, living together in a family group. The family consists of one stallion with six to ten mares, foals and yearlings. Each animal has its place in the social order of the group. The stallion is the "chief". When the family goes on treks across the plains, his job is to protect the rear. He keeps intruders at bay and chases any foals that get left behind. The senior ranking mare leads the group, with the other members and their foals following behind in order of rank.

Several family groups may graze together, sleep together or join up into herds of several thousand animals when migrating. They migrate in order to find new, fresh areas on which to graze. It has been known for mixed herds of Grant's and Grévy's zebras to graze together, but they do not seem to mate with each other.

Zebra mares can reproduce when only two years old. Breeding can happen at any time of year, although bad conditions, like a drought or food shortage, may reduce the desire to mate. A healthy mare may bear up to six foals in her lifetime. Foals are born one at a time.

A Burchell zebra foal is born after 371 days. It is a dusty shade with stripes, and is about the size and weight of a new-born donkey foal. Shortly after the birth the mother gets to her feet and licks her foal dry. This licking also acts as a massage to circulate the blood of the tiny foal, and to make a bond of recognition between mare and foal.

After perhaps half an hour, the foal will struggle to its feet and stand on very wobbly legs. Then it begins to feed from its mother. The mare's milk contains a pink substance called colostrum. This protects the foal against disease and helps its bowels to work. The mare will suckle the foal for up to twelve months, as long as her milk lasts. If she is in foal again, she will probably suckle for only six months. After about ten days, the foal will begin to graze, as well as feeding from its mother.

For one reason or another, only about half the zebra foals born survive and live to maturity. The rest die from weakness of lack of milk from the mother, or are attacked and killed by predators. Young zebras, like all young wild animals, are very obedient to their superiors. The ranking order is quite clear, and strictly obeyed. This is one reason for the smooth running of a herd animal's life. The young know they must behave according to the rules of the herd and do what they are told.

Although the family groups are usually peaceable, fights sometimes break out between the stallions. This often happens when an ambitious colt wants to steal a mare or filly from the herd and begin a family of his own. The herd stallion threatens the intruder, stretching out his neck, head and ears forward. Then he opens his mouth and lays his ears back. If the colt

retreats, all is well. But if he is willing to fight, he too approaches with open mouth and ears laid back. Both males attack by biting each other's throat, neck, mouth or forehead. They may circle to bite the other's hind-quarters. Or they may turn and kick with their powerful hind legs. When one of them knows he is beaten, he lowers his head sideways to show it.

4
Friends and Enemies

The zebra's closest companion, and the most helpful, is the oxpecker bird. You can see several of these little birds sitting on the back of these zebras. They travel along with the zebras and pick out the tiresome insects which infest their coats and make them itch.

To us, the zebra is a beautiful, gentle wild horse. But to many animals of Africa it makes a splendid meal. Zebras have many enemies and predators, from the jackal, spotted hyena and lion to the fierce hunting dogs that roam the savannah. These dogs hunt in packs and run their prey down until it is exhausted and comes to a standstill. The dogs attack from the rear and will devour a zebra in a very short time.

Humans are the zebra's worst enemy. We have hunted the zebra for its skin and killed it for sport. Some zebra species, such as the Grévy and mountain zebras, have been reduced to only a few thousand. There are about 300,000 Burchell's zebras left, although these may be increasing. Bush fires are also a hazard of which zebras and many other wild animals are afraid. In the face of this danger, herds of many different animals join together in flight.

In many ways the zebra is well adapted to the life that nature has provided. Its striped coat breaks up its outline in the distance and provides a natural disguise. It can, when necessary, cover distances at speed to escape from its enemies. It eats well on the sometimes sparse savannah or mountain grasses. Its senses of sight, hearing and smell are very acute and help protect it from its enemies. Only hunters, both animal and human, threaten its peaceful life.

Fortunately, there are wild animal reserves in Africa where animals are safe from the selfishness of humans. Perhaps the best-known is the Serengeti National Park. But no-one should sit back and think that the future of the zebra is safe. The quagga, another relative of the wild horse and zebra, has become extinct during the past hundred years after being ruthlessly hunted on the South African veldt.

Today we know more about the dangers of extinction. Our zoos and wild life parks, and the reserves in Africa, strive to protect any animal that may be endangered. Once a species has disappeared, however, it can never be revived. We should remember that the futures of the Przewalsky horses and the mountain zebras are far from secure.

It is the end of a hot day on the African plains. The zebras are slowly making their way in the evening light to their chosen resting place. They will sleep, secure in the knowledge that one or two members of the herd will keep guard and warn them of any approaching danger.

Next morning, as dawn breaks, the whole struggle for survival will begin all over again. There will be water and food to find, enemies to watch for, companions to meet at the water holes. This life cycle will go on for the zebras for just as long as mankind sees that it is not destroyed.

Glossary

COLOSTRUM A pink substance found in mares' milk for 3 to 4 days after giving birth.

COLT A young male horse or zebra.

DORSAL STRIPE Also called an eel stripe; a black or brown stripe running along the back of a wild horse or zebra to the tail.

EVOLUTION Gradual change in shape, form and behaviour over a long period of time.

EXTINCT Died out—no longer living.

FILLY A young mare.

FOREHAND Shoulders and front legs.

HABITAT Type of place where a particular animal usually lives.

HIND-QUARTERS The hind legs, rump and tail of an animal.

NOMADS Wandering tribes of natives.

PAMPAS Large open plain.

PREDATORS Animals that hunt and eat others.

PRZEWALSKY Wild horse of Mongolia, so called after Colonel N. M. Przewalsky, a Russian who discovered them in 1883.

SAVANNAH Wide, flat land covered with low bushes and small clumps of trees.

SEDGE Grass-like plant which grows in marshes and by the waterside.

SPECIES Group of similar animals that inter-breed.

STALLION An adult male horse or zebra.

STEPPE Dry, grassy, uncultivated plain.

VELDT Open grassland in South Africa.

WITHERS The ridge between the shoulder bones of a horse.

YEARLING A one-year-old animal.

Further Reading

Groves, Dr Colin P., *Horses, Asses and Zebras* (David and Charles, 1975).

May, J., *The First Horses* (Blackie, 1970).

Mohr, Dr Erna, *The Asiatic Wild Horse* (J. A. Allen, 1971).

Ryden, Hope, *Wild Horses* (Secker & Warburg, 1972).

Atlas of World Wildlife (Mitchell Beazley, 1973).

The Living World of Animals (Reader's Digest, 1970).

ACKNOWLEDGMENTS

The author and publisher would like to thank the following for their permission to reproduce copyright illustrations on the pages mentioned: N.H.P.A., 6, 7, 10, 11, 14, 16-17, 18-19, 20, 25, 30, 35, 40, 41, 44-45, 49 (Peter Johnson), endpapers (R. H. Smith), 15 (Anthony Bannister), 24, 32-33 (K. B. Newman), 38 (J. Good); Ecology Pictures, 4-5, 21, 36, 37, 42-43, 50 (Peter Ward), 13, 52-53 (M. P. L. Fogden), 23, 48, 51 (David C. Houston); Bruce Coleman, 8 (Mark Boulton), 26, 27, jacket back (Jane Burton), 46, jacket front (Norman Myers); Heather Angel, 28-29.
The map and diagram on p. 9 were drawn by Celia Ware.

Index